"Kevin lays out an [...] disciplemaking that re[...] Instead of prescriptively telling people what to believe, *First Things* crafts core conversations while exploring biblical truth and has become a proven method for spiritual formation."

**David Robbins**,
CEO and President of FamilyLife

"I have used *First Things* for 10 years, both in campus ministry and as a pastor, and I haven't found anything as clear, comprehensive, and transferable. I commend it to anyone wanting to take the next step in discipleship."

**Jim Davis**,
Executive Pastor, Grace Bible Church, Oxford, Mississippi

"*First Things* is an excellent resource that lets the Word of God speak for itself. It is great for those who are seeking to investigate Christianity as well as believers seeking a firm, biblical foundation for their faith."

**Josh Shideler**,
Campus Director of Cru at Mississippi State University

# First Things

## SURVEYING THE BASICS OF THE BIBLE

### KEVIN SHOEMAKER

LUCIDBOOKS

**First Things**
Surveying the Basics of the Bible
Copyright © 2017 by Kevin Shoemaker

Published by Lucid Books in Houston, TX
www.LucidBooksPublishing.com

All rights reserved. No part of this publication may be reproduced, stored in a retrieval system, or transmitted in any form by any means, electronic, mechanical, photocopy, recording, or otherwise, without the prior permission of the publisher, except as provided for by USA copyright law.

Scripture quotations are from the ESV® Bible (The Holy Bible, English Standard Version®), copyright © 2001 by Crossway, a publishing ministry of Good News Publishers. Used by permission. All rights reserved.

ISBN-10: 1-63296-171-7
ISBN-13: 978-1-63296-171-6
eISBN-10: 1-63296-172-5
eISBN-13: 978-1-63296-172-3

Special Sales: Most Lucid Books titles are available in special quantity discounts. Custom imprinting or excerpting can also be done to fit special needs. Contact Lucid Books at Info@LucidBooksPublishing.com.

*Dedicated to Randy Phillips*
*(1957–2013)*

*The grass withers, the flower fades,*
*but the word of our God will stand forever.*
*Isaiah 40:8*

# TABLE OF CONTENTS

# THE META-NARRATIVE

*"The theme of the Bible is the kingdom of God. That is where the biblical account both starts and finishes. Salvation is the means by which the sovereign God brings sinful people into that kingdom as its willing and acceptable subjects."*

—Graeme Goldsworthy

In order to best understand the message of the Bible, one must understand the kingdom of God. Every verse in the Bible has a context, a part in a bigger story. Even more, each book of the Bible has a context; in fact, all books of the Bible combine to bring about one, big, unified story in which a hero comes to restore his kingdom by sacrificing himself for the good of his people. One way of understanding this big story is by dividing it into four parts: creation, fall, redemption, and restoration.

**Creation (Genesis 1 & 2)**
In the beginning God created the world and everything in it. He commanded Adam and Eve to increase numerically, expand geographically, and to rule the world with him (Genesis 1:28). In this, God was creating a kingdom on earth.

**Fall (Genesis 3)**
However, Adam and Eve were deceived by Satan and

rejected God's plan for them to rule the world together. Because of this choice, they had to leave God's kingdom and a curse was put on all of mankind. However, God promised that one day a savior would redeem mankind from the power of Satan, bringing God's people back into his kingdom.

### Redemption (Genesis 3:15–Revelation 20)

The story of mankind being redeemed and brought back into the kingdom of God on earth hinges on the life, death, and resurrection of Jesus Christ. The work of Jesus is the catalyst for the redemption of all things. The Old Testament prepares the way for Jesus, and the New Testament introduces Jesus and instructs his people in how to take part in his redemptive plan.

### Restoration (Revelation 21 & 22)

Through the redemptive work of Jesus, the kingdom of God on earth is being restored and will one day be fully restored. As we await the return of Jesus and the full restoration of the kingdom of God on earth, we participate in the kingdom by submitting ourselves to King Jesus and his ways, that his will might be done and that his kingdom would come (Matthew 6:10).

The purpose of this introduction is to explain how the meta-narrative of the Bible focuses on the kingdom of God.

If one were to think of the Bible as a forest, the kingdom of God would be the forest and the many teachings it gives would be the trees. Many times, the grand story of the Bible can be lost by focusing only on more detailed teachings. However, as the saying goes, "One shouldn't miss the forest for the trees." Therefore, with the forest in mind we will examine some of the trees in this glorious story of the good news of the kingdom of God.

This booklet is meant to be understood as an abridged systematic theology. Wayne Grudem defines systematic theology as "any study that answers the question, 'What does the whole Bible teach us today?' about any given topic." There will be questions followed by scripture references, with no written answers by the author. That will enable the reader or group to "examine the scriptures" themselves (Acts 17:11), ask the Lord for wisdom (James 1:5), and think it over to let the Lord give understanding (2 Timothy 2:7).

# RECONCILIATION

*"The Christian Gospel is that I am so flawed that Jesus had to die for me, yet I am so loved and valued that Jesus was glad to die for me. This leads to deep humility and deep confidence at the same time. It undermines both swaggering and sniveling. I cannot feel superior to anyone, and yet I have nothing to prove to anyone."*

—Tim Keller

What does God require from us?
- Exodus 20:3–17 (The 10 Commandments)
- James 2:10

What are the consequences of not meeting those requirements?
- Romans 5:12
- Galatians 3:10
- Matthew 13:40–42

What did Jesus do for us?
- Isaiah 53:5–6
- Romans 5:6–8
- Galatians 3:10–13
- Matthew 20:28

How can we be reconciled to God?
- John 3:16–18
- Romans 5:1–2
- Galatians 2:16
- Ephesians 2:8–9

How can we know if our faith is genuine and we are living under God's grace?
- 2 Corinthians 5:17
- Ephesians 4:20–24

How can we know if our faith is not genuine and we are still living under God's wrath?
- Hebrews 10:26–27
- James 2:17–19
- 1 John 3:9

How should we respond if we believe that Jesus died and rose again for us?
- Acts 2:37–41

# RESURRECTION

*"Jesus's resurrection is the beginning of God's new project not to snatch people away from earth to heaven but to colonize earth with the life of heaven. That, after all, is what the Lord's Prayer is about."*

—N.T. Wright

What did Jesus say would happen after his death?
– Mark 9:31

What will happen after the death of Christians?
– 1 Corinthians 15:35–53
– Philippians 3:20–21

What will happen to non-Christians at the resurrection?
– Daniel 12:2
– John 5:28–29

Will death be put to death?
– Luke 20:36
– John 11:25–26
– 1 Corinthians 15:26
– 1 Corinthians 15:54–57

Will heaven come to earth?
– Revelation 21:1–4

What are the implications if there is no resurrection?
– 1 Corinthians 15:12–19

How should the resurrection encourage us?
– 1 Thessalonians 4:13–18

# LAW & GRACE

*"Without a heart transformed by the grace of Christ, we just continue to manage external and internal darkness."*

—Matt Chandler

What is the purpose of the law in regards to salvation?
- Romans 3:19–20
- Romans 5:20
- Romans 7:5, 7–8, 13

How does someone become righteous in God's sight?
- Romans 3:21–22
- Romans 4:3–6
- 2 Corinthians 5:21
- Philippians 3:8–9

Can someone lose their salvation?
- John 6:38–40
- John 10:27–29
- Hebrews 10:14

What about those who turn away from the faith?
- 1 John 2:19

What should our motivation be in regards to obeying God's commands?
- Titus 2:11–12
- 2 Corinthians 5:14–15
- Luke 7:41–47

How should we respond when we sin?
- 1 John 1:5–10

# HOLY SPIRIT

*"Without the Spirit we can neither love God nor keep His commandments."*

—St. Augustine

Where is it implied that the Holy Spirit is God?
– Genesis 1:1–2
– Matthew 28:19

What role does the Holy Spirit play in being born again?
– John 3:5–8

Where does the Holy Spirit dwell?
– Romans 8:9–11
– 1 Corinthians 3:16

What is the function of the Holy Spirit?
– Ezekiel 36:25–27
– John 16:13–14
– 1 Corinthians 2:11–12
– 1 Corinthians 12:1–11
– Galatians 5:22–23

What are we commanded to do in regards to the Holy Spirit?

- Romans 8:5–7
- Galatians 5:16
- Ephesians 5:18

# SCRIPTURE

*"The primary purpose of reading the Bible is not to know the Bible but to know God."*

—James Merritt

By what authority do the Scriptures speak?
- 2 Timothy 3:16

Are the Scriptures without error (inerrant)?
- Psalm 119:160

Can the Scriptures be understood by the common person?
- Psalm 19:7
- Psalm 119:130

Who cannot understand the Scriptures?
- 1 Corinthians 1:18–21
- 1 Corinthians 2:14
- 2 Corinthians 4:3–4

Are the Scriptures sufficient for knowing all God wants us to think or know?
- 2 Timothy 3:14–17
- Deuteronomy 29:29

What are the Scriptures about?
- Luke 24:44
- John 1:45
- John 5:39–40

What role do the Scriptures play in being born again?
- 2 Timothy 3:15
- 1 Peter 1:23

Why should I read the Scriptures?
- Psalm 119:165
- John 8:31–34
- John 14:21
- John 17:17
- 2 Timothy 3:16–17

In reading the Scriptures, what do we need to be careful to do?
- Matthew 7:24–27
- James 1:22–25

# FELLOWSHIP

*"In the New Testament, we don't find our gift through self-examination and introspection and then find ways to express it. Instead, we love one another, serve one another, help one another, and in so doing we see how God has equipped us to do so."*

—Russell Moore

How should Christians treat one another?
- John 13:34
- Romans 12:10
- Romans 15:5
- Romans 15:14
- Galatians 5:13–14
- Galatians 6:2
- Ephesians 4:2
- Colossians 3:13
- Hebrews 10:24–25
- James 5:16
- 1 Peter 4:9–10

How should Christians not treat one another?
- Galatians 5:15, 26
- Ephesians 4:26–27
- Colossians 3:9
- James 4:11

– James 5:9

Are there consequences to the company we keep?
– Proverbs 13:20
– 1 Corinthians 15:33

Does this mean we should not associate with non-Christians?
– Matthew 5:13–16
– Colossians 4:5

# GOOD WORKS

*"Abhor all idea of being saved by good works, but O, be as full of good works as if you were to be saved by them!"*

—Charles Spurgeon

Are good works by Christians random or prepared by God?
– Ephesians 2:10

What did Jesus redeem his people to be?
– Titus 2:11–14

What should we be devoted to?
– Titus 3:8, 14

How should Christians encourage one another?
– Hebrews 10:24

Should our good works toward others be noticeable?
– Matthew 5:14–16
– Matthew 6:1–4

Why does God give some Christians wealth?
– 1 Timothy 6:17–19

What does it look like to be "spiritual" or "religious" but lacking in good works?

- Isaiah 58:1–10
- James 1:26–27
- James 2:14–17

What does it mean if someone professes faith in God, but lacks good works as evidence?

  - Titus 1:16

How is wisdom revealed in others?

- James 3:13

# THE CHURCH

*"Being united to Christ means being united to every Christian. But that universal union must be given a living, breathing existence in a local church."*

—Mark Dever

Whom did Christ die for?
– Ephesians 5:25

Who represents Christ on earth?
– Ephesians 1:22–23

Who is building the church?
– Matthew 16:18

What metaphors do the Scriptures use to describe the church?
– 1 Corinthians 3:6–9
– 1 Corinthians 12:12–27
– Ephesians 5:31–32
– 1 Timothy 3:15
– Hebrews 3:6
– 1 Peter 2:5

Who leads the church?
- 1 Timothy 3:1–7
- Titus 1:5–9
- Hebrews 13:7, 17

What is the mission of the church?
- Matthew 28:18–20

What is church discipline?
- Matthew 18:15–20
- 1 Corinthians 5:9–13

# THE GREAT COMMISSION

*"We must be global Christians with a global vision because our God is a global God."*

—John R.W. Stott

What is the Great Commission?
- Matthew 28:18–20

What task has God given to his people?
- Mark 16:15
- Luke 4:43 (John 20:21)
- 2 Corinthians 5:18–20

What did Jesus encourage his disciples to pray for in regards to this task?
- Matthew 9:36–38
- Luke 10:1–2

Why does God "send out laborers"?
- Acts 20:24
- Acts 26:18
- Romans 10:14–17
- 1 Corinthians 1:17
- 2 Corinthians 4:1–7
- 2 Corinthians 5:20

What does this work look like?
- Luke 8:4–8, 11–15
- 1 Corinthians 3:5–9

What is the ultimate purpose for God sending laborers?
- Psalm 86:9
- Revelation 7:9–10

# EVANGELISM

*"Success in witnessing is simply taking the initiative to share Christ in the power of the Holy Spirit and leaving the results to God."*

—Bill Bright

What is God's role in evangelism?
– John 6:44
– John 6:65

What is a Christian's role in evangelism?
– Matthew 10:16
– Matthew 28:18–20
– Romans 10:13–17
– 2 Corinthians 5:11, 18–20

How does the Bible characterize unbelievers?
– John 3:19–20
– Romans 1:21
– Romans 8:7–8
– 2 Corinthians 4:4
– Ephesians 4:18

What happens when a person becomes a Christian?
– John 3:3
– Romans 8:1

## Evangelism

- 2 Corinthians 5:17
- Colossians 1:13–14
- 1 Peter 2:25

# PRAYER

*"Self-will and prayer are both ways of getting things done. At the center of self-will is me, carving a world in my image, but at the center of prayer is God, carving me in his Son's image."*

—Paul Miller

How should we pray?
- Matthew 6:5–13
- Luke 11:5–13
- Luke 18:1–8

What conditions are required in receiving our requests from God?
- Psalm 66:18
- Matthew 21:22
- John 14:13–14
- John 15:7
- James 4:3
- 1 John 3:22
- 1 John 5:14

What are some examples of answered prayer?
- 1 Kings 3:5–12
- Isaiah 38:1–5
- James 5:17–18

When should I pray?
- Psalm 5:3
- Psalm 55:17
- Daniel 6:10
- 1 Thessalonians 5:17

What promises do we have in prayer?
- Matthew 7:7–11
- Philippians 4:6–7
- Hebrews 4:15–16
- James 1:5

# FAMILY

*"It has been said that as goes the family, so goes the world. It can also be said that as goes the father, so goes the family."*

—Voddie Baucham Jr.

What does the Bible say about a Christian marrying a non-Christian?
- 2 Corinthians 6:14–15

What does the Bible say about the husband's role?
- 1 Corinthians 11:3
- Ephesians 5:25–31
- Colossians 3:19
- 1 Timothy 5:8
- 1 Peter 3:7

What does the Bible say about the wife's role?
- Genesis 2:18
- Ephesians 5:22–24
- Ephesians 5:33
- Colossians 3:18
- Titus 2:3–5
- 1 Peter 3:1–6
- Proverbs 21:19

What does the Bible say about the parent's responsibility?
- Deuteronomy 6:6–7
- Psalm 78:4–7
- Proverbs 22:6
- Proverbs 22:15
- Proverbs 29:15, 17
- Ephesians 6:4
- Colossians 3:21

What does the Bible say about divorce?
- Matthew 5:31–32
- Matthew 19:3–9
- Mark 10:2–12
- Luke 16:18
- Romans 7:2–3
- 1 Corinthians 7:10–16
- 1 Corinthians 7:39

# PRIDE & HUMILITY

*"Pride makes us artificial and humility makes us real."*

—Thomas Merton

How does the Bible contrast the proud and humble?
- Psalm 18:27
- Psalm 138:6
- Proverbs 18:12
- Proverbs 29:23
- James 4:6

What are some examples of God opposing the proud?
- Exodus 10:3–6
- 2 Chronicles 33:10–13
- Daniel 4:28–33
- Daniel 5:18–21
- Acts 12:21–23

How does God give grace to the humble?
- 2 Chronicles 32:24–26
- 2 Chronicles 34:26–28
- Proverbs 15:33
- Isaiah 57:15
- Isaiah 66:2

What did Jesus say about the proud and the humble?
- Matthew 23:1–12
- Luke 14:7–11
- Luke 18:9–14

How does a person become prideful?
- Deuteronomy 8:11–18

# ETERNITY & REWARDS

*"Whatever good thing you do for Him, if done according to the Word, is laid up for you as treasure in chests and coffers, to be brought out to be rewarded before both men and angels, to your eternal comfort."*

—John Bunyan

What does the Bible say about our lifespan?
- Job 9:25–26
- Job 14:1–2
- Psalm 39:5
- James 4:14

What does the Bible say about rewards?
- Matthew 6:1–5, 16
- Matthew 6:19–21
- Matthew 10:40–42
- Luke 6:35
- Luke 14:12–14
- 1 Corinthians 3:12–15
- Ephesians 6:5–8
- Hebrews 11:6

How does the Bible describe eternal life for believers?
- Luke 23:42–43

- John 14:1–3
- Revelation 21:3–5, 22–27
- Revelation 22:1–5

How does the Bible describe judgment for unbelievers?
- Matthew 13:40–42, 47–50
- Matthew 25:41
- Luke 16:19–31
- Revelation 21:8

What is the Great White Throne Judgment?
- Revelation 20:11–15

What is the Judgment Seat of Christ?
- 2 Corinthians 5:6–12

How should what the Bible teaches about eternity and rewards change our perspectives on our lives?
- Psalm 90:12
- Philippians 1:21–24

# ANGELS & DEMONS

*"There is no neutral ground in the universe; every square inch, every split second, is claimed by God and counter-claimed by Satan."*

—C.S. Lewis

What role do angels play in the lives of believers?
- Hebrews 1:14
- Daniel 3:27–28
- Daniel 6:22
- Matthew 18:10

Are there unseen powers working against believers?
- Ephesians 6:11–12

What does Satan do?
- Genesis 2:15–17; 3:1–6
- Luke 8:11–12
- John 8:44
- 2 Corinthians 4:4
- 2 Corinthians 11:3
- 2 Corinthians 11:13–15
- 1 Peter 5:8

What is the ultimate end of Satan?
- Matthew 25:41
- John 12:31
- Romans 16:20
- Revelation 20:10


How do we fight against the work of Satan?
- Ephesians 6:10–18

# MONEY

*"God created us to love people and use things, but materialists love
things and use people."*

—Randy Alcorn

What warnings does the Bible give in regards to money?
- Psalm 62:10
- Ecclesiastes 5:10
- Matthew 6:19–21
- Luke 12:13–21
- Luke 16:10–13
- 1 Timothy 6:8–10, 17
- Hebrews 13:5

What belongs to God?
- Job 41:11
- Psalm 24:1
- Psalm 50:10–12

Who should be given to?
- Proverbs 21:13
- Ezekiel 16:49
- 1 Corinthians 9:14
- 2 Corinthians 8:13–15
- Galatians 2:10

- Galatians 6:6
- 1 Timothy 5:3–4
- 1 Timothy 5:8
- 1 Timothy 5:17–18
- 3 John 1:5–8

Why is it that "those who proclaim the gospel should get their living by the gospel"?
- 1 Corinthians 9:7

What should be our motivation in giving to the poor?
- 2 Corinthians 8:9

What blessings are promised in giving?
- Proverbs 3:9–10
- Proverbs 11:24–25
- Proverbs 19:17
- Proverbs 28:27
- Luke 6:38
- 2 Corinthians 9:6, 10–13

How should we give?
- 2 Corinthians 9:7

What caution does the Bible tell us about giving?
- Matthew 6:1–4

# WORDS

*"The true test of a man's spirituality is not his ability to speak, as we are apt to think, but rather his ability to bridle his tongue."*
—R. Kent Hughes

How does the Bible encourage us to use our words?
- Proverbs 16:24
- Matthew 5:37
- Ephesians 4:29
- Colossians 4:6
- 1 Thessalonians 5:11, 14
- Hebrews 3:13
- Hebrews 10:24–25

How does the Bible discourage us to use our words?
- Proverbs 11:13
- Proverbs 15:1
- Proverbs 16:28
- Proverbs 18:2
- Proverbs 18:8
- Proverbs 20:19
- Proverbs 27:2
- Proverbs 29:20
- Proverbs 30:10
- Colossians 3:8

- 1 Timothy 6:4–5
- James 5:12
- 1 Peter 2:1

What does the Bible say about withholding our words?
- Proverbs 10:19
- Proverbs 12:23
- Proverbs 17:27
- Proverbs 17:28
- Proverbs 18:13
- Proverbs 21:23
- Ecclesiastes 5:1–2
- Ecclesiastes 6:11
- James 1:19
- James 1:26

# CHRISTIAN LIBERTY

*"A Christian is a perfectly free lord of all, subject to none. A Christian is a perfectly dutiful servant of all, subject to all."*

—Martin Luther

Read the following verse and consider how it inspired the above quote by Martin Luther.

- 1 Corinthians 9:19

Read 1 Corinthians 10:23–24.

- What does this mean?

In 1 Corinthians 10 Paul is addressing the issue of whether or not it is permissible to eat meat that has been sacrificed or dedicated to idols. Some said it was impermissible because of its association with idolatry, while others understood it to be simply meat that ultimately comes from the Lord and therefore permissible. How does Paul address this issue?

- 1 Corinthians 10:25–33

In Romans 14 Paul is addressing a difference of opinions again over what Christians believe is permissible or impermissible to eat. This issue came about as the people of God transitioned from the Old Covenant, with its food restrictions, to the New

Covenant, which did not include food restrictions. Some believing Jews struggled with the freedom to eat the food that was formerly prohibited, but now was not prohibited under the New Covenant. How does Paul address this issue?

– Romans 14:1–4

How does Paul address Christians in disagreement over non-essential issues?

– Romans 14:5–12

What should we pursue when there are disagreements over non-essential issues?

– Romans 14:13, 15, 19

What should a Christian do who feels at liberty to do something that another "weaker brother" might view as sin?

– Romans 14:15–16, 20–22

What obligation do we have in regards to obeying our conscience?

– Romans 14:14, 23

What is the kingdom of God about?

– Romans 14:17

# ALCOHOL

*"Let there be no drunkenness; for wine is the work of God, but drunkenness is the work of the devil. Wine makes not drunkenness; but intemperance produces it. Do not accuse that which is the workmanship of God, but accuse the madness of a fellow mortal."*

—John Chrysostom

What does the Bible prohibit in regards to alcohol?
- Romans 13:1–2, 5
- Ephesians 5:18
- 1 Peter 4:3

Outside of what the Bible prohibits, should we judge others on this issue?
- Romans 14:1–4
- Romans 14:10, 12
- Romans 14:22
- 1 Corinthians 5:12

How should we respond to our conscience in regards to drinking alcohol?
- Romans 14:5, 14, 23

If someone is of legal age, not getting drunk, and has a clear conscience in regards to drinking alcohol, is there any other reason for them not to drink?
– Romans 14:13, 15–16, 20–21

What other warnings does the Bible give in regards to alcohol?
– Proverbs 20:1
– Proverbs 23:29–35

# SEXUAL IMMORALITY

*"The strongest Christian is unsafe among occasions to sin."*

—Richard Baxter

Where does sexual immorality come from?
- Matthew 15:19
- Mark 7:21

What commands does the Bible give in regards to sexual immorality?
- 1 Corinthians 6:18
- Colossians 3:5
- 1 Thessalonians 4:3–5

Where should we draw the line to "flee," "put to death," and to "abstain" from sexual immorality?
- Romans 13:13–14
- 1 Corinthians 6:20
- Ephesians 5:3
- 1 Timothy 5:1–2

How should we respond to a Christian who is living in sexual immorality?
- Galatians 6:1
- Matthew 18:15–17

– 1 Corinthians 5:9–13

How should we respond to a non-Christian living in sexual immorality?
– 1 Corinthians 5:9–10, 12–13

What does the Bible say about homosexuality?
– Leviticus 18:22
– Romans 1:24–27
– 1 Corinthians 6:9–10
– 1 Timothy 1:8–11

What warnings does the Bible give about adultery?
– Proverbs 2:16–19
– Proverbs 5:20–23
– Proverbs 6:32
– Proverbs 7:1–27
– Proverbs 9:17–18
– Ecclesiastes 7:25–26
– Hebrews 13:4

# ACCOUNTABILITY

*"Nothing can be more cruel than the leniency which abandons others to their sin. Nothing can be more compassionate than the severe reprimand which calls another Christian in one's community back from the path of sin."*

—Dietrich Bonhoeffer

What standards are Christians accountable to?
- 1 Peter 1:15–16
- 2 Corinthians 7:1
- 1 Thessalonians 4:7

What encouragement do we have to hold others accountable?
- Proverbs 27:5–6
- Proverbs 28:23
- Galatians 6:1

What should this process look like?
- 2 Timothy 3:16
- Matthew 18:15–17
- Luke 17:3–4

What about being judgmental?
- Matthew 7:1–5
- 1 Corinthians 5:12

What would validate church discipline?

- Matthew 18:17
- 1 Corinthians 5:9–13
- Titus 3:10–11

# ACKNOWLEDGMENTS

My deep thanks to those who have helped me along the way to create *First Things: Surveying the Basics of the Bible.*

I will be forever grateful to Randy Phillips, to whom this book is dedicated. Randy took the time to meet with me not only to study the Bible, but to teach me to seek the Lord through the Scriptures. This book also has the fingerprints of many staff and students with Cru at Mississippi State, whose feedback over the years helped refine and expand this work. The Lord has further blessed me with a band of brothers and sisters at Redeemer Church who have called, encouraged, and enabled me to study and teach the Word of God. Finally, I would like to thank my wife, Missy, whose honesty and sincerity helps me better know the Lord and be a better man.

CPSIA information can be obtained
at www.ICGtesting.com
Printed in the USA
LVOW10s0002091217
559186LV00007B/173/P